One step at a Time

Mourning a Child

Betty Madill

Blue Butterfly Publishers Ltd

First published 1997 by Papillion Publishing, Inverurie under the title *Sowing the Seeds of Hope*

Revised edition published 2001 by Floris Books, Edinburgh, Scotland

Second revised edition published October 2011 by Blue Butterfly Publishers.

This edition published December 2015 by Blue Butterfly Publishers Ltd, also available as an eBook on most devices.

Betty Madill©2015

ISBN 978-0-9573670-3-6

Front cover image supplied by F Madill Photography
2014©FionaMadill
www.facebook/fmadillphotography

Back cover images supplied by Shuttlestock

Dedication

To all bereaved parents throughout the world grieving the death of their beloved children.

With a special thank you to Patsy for her help and advice

Contents

Introduction

May the Lord answer you
When you are in trouble!
Psalm 20:1

When we lose a child, part of us dies too. No one can see the inner piece that is missing. No medicine, no bandaging and no amount of counselling can make us whole again.

Only a bereaved parent knows, deep within, the part that will never mend and the scars left on heart and soul.

Since we cannot go back to a life which our child was so much a part, we must somehow go forward every day, little by little, into a future without them but not devoid of them.

No one can take away from us the memories of our children. But instead of living only with regret, let us celebrate the fact that they were ours, and will always be so, that through them we met life head on. We will always miss them and this is only natural, but we can never lose them again.

Through this book I hope to encourage bereaved parents, as well as their close friends and family, to share those treasured memories. To allow us to talk about our children, whenever and wherever, as we wish. To permit us to weep together, if necessary, and to hold each other close when we cannot find words to say. It is also, most of all, to give us as much time as we require to mourn our precious children, and not to have to follow `norms' which are alien to us.

The aims of this book may seem too high for some bereaved parents to contemplate, but bear with me and we shall walk the road together. Don't run, take your time, put the book down when it becomes too heavy. It will still be there when you are strong enough to continue. The road is rough with many hidden potholes, but it is open to all who take one step at a time.

No Death So Sad, a leaflet published by The Compassionate Friends TCF a support movement for bereaved parents, reports that over fifteen thousand children and young people die each year in Britain, which works out at about 288 every week of the year.

From these figures, it can be seen that we are not alone. While there are many mothers and fathers helping each other to cope, many more are doing so on their own, without any awareness that they do not have to deal with their tragedy in isolation. They have no one to advise them where to go for support should they need it. This is why support movements like TCF and CRUSE can help and they can be found all over the world. This is also why books like this one are written to highlight the issues faced by bereaved people.

Monday 7th February, 1983

My husband Dave and I spent that Sunday, the 6th together in our apartment with the children — three-year old Lisa and fourteen-month old Kevin — not doing very much. It was one of those family days you wish you could capture and hold in your mind. I suppose in some way I have held on to it, due to the events that were to occur the next morning more in for any other reason.

We had by then lived in Rio de Janeiro, Brazil, for almost two years. In the southern hemisphere February is summertime and the weather that weekend was lovely — hot without being oppressive, with a light, cooling breeze.

Our apartment was on the fifth floor of a block of flats. It had a balcony that was very secure and an ideal place for the children to play on. This is where my two were playing that Sunday. I would look up from my book to check on them from time to time. For a change they were playing without their usual squabbling.

I can still recall the feelings of well-being I had that day, absorbing the lovely atmosphere which seemed to surround us. As things turned out it was the calm before the storm.

The next day, Monday, I was woken by the phone ringing by my bedside. I had been having such a lovely sleep, that I hesitated to answer it. But in case it might be important, I picked up the receiver.

It was my friend, Susan, calling to invite me out to her place, so that our children could play together, Lisa and Daniel, Susan's little son who was six months younger, were great friends. I agreed to accept Susan's offer.

I went through to Lisa's bedroom and found her still fast asleep. I hesitated to wake her, but as it was such a beautiful sunny day, I decided she'd be much better outside, instead of lying in bed. When I shook her and told her where we were going, she jumped up, full of anticipation at the thought of seeing her friend, Daniel.

We ate breakfast, and then went through to wash and dress. While I was getting Lisa ready, I couldn't help noticing how much she had grown during the summer months. I remember thinking she had finally left her babyhood behind, and was now a proper little girl.

Of all my children, Lisa had the fairest hair and blue eyes. That morning her hair never looked as blond and her blue eyes sparkled. I am so glad that I noticed these things. Otherwise I might have imagined later that I'd made them up.

We were soon in the car heading for Susan's house I had decided to leave Kevin with my daily help, Yara. He was still asleep anyway. It was better to leave him to wake by himself, as he always liked sleeping late in the mornings.

When we arrived at Susan's, she already had a pot of tea in front of her on the patio table. She poured me a cup, while the two children ran indoors to play. We chatted idly, catching up with the latest gossip, and since we were sitting outside, the children soon came back to play beside us in the garden.

Even though it was not long after ten in the morning, the sun was already pretty hot. To cool the children down, just a few feet from us we put out a small paddling-pool so they could splash about in the water. The main aim behind this idea was to keep the children away from the swimming-pool which was part of the front garden.

Susan's fifteen-month old son Luke had woken and was crying for attention. While she went up to fetch him down, I decided to check on the other two. Since I couldn't hear them in the garden, I went to look for them in the house.

While I was still looking, I heard Susan outside shouting over and over again: "Lisa is in the water, Lisa is in the water!" There was great panic in her voice. I went straight to the poolside and stood there completely transfixed. There was my beautiful Lisa, lying on the floor of the pool, as if she were sound a sleep

Then Susan's handyman Billy suddenly appeared from the back of the house where he had been working, alarmed by all the commotion. He immediately jumped into the water and pulled Lisa out.

Susan tried mouth-to-mouth resuscitation on Lisa. All I could do was stand and watch and pray. I prayed for her to be revived, and then I prayed for help to survive if she wasn't.

Susan sent me to phone our husbands, who worked together in the same office, some six miles away in another part of the city. As soon as they realized the seriousness of the situation they headed home.

While I was phoning, Billy ran with Lisa in his arms, to a medical centre nearby.
The doctors tried very hard to revive Lisa. I am sure they did their best, but to no avail. When Dave arrived at the medical centre, I had to be the one to tell him the sad news that Lisa was dead.

I had set out to spend a pleasant morning chatting to a dear friend, while our children played together in the sunshine. Just four hours later, I was to return home, without my precious little girl.

To this day I do not understand what made Lisa go to the pool. She had never done so before on the many occasions we had visited Susan. Both Daniel and Lisa seemed content enough to play with the toys we had given them.

Lisa did ask me for the inflatable ring that was on the table, but I explained to her that it was the baby's, and he would need it when Susan brought him downstairs to play. How often I have wondered: would she still be here had I given her that ring? Would it have been enough to help her stay afloat?

Some years later, I learned that toddlers below a certain age do not struggle when immersed in water, and that they simply breathe the water into their lungs. This would account for why neither Susan nor I heard Lisa in the pool. There was no sound to hear; therefore she slowly, silently drowned.

Premonition

When I set off to visit my friend that beautiful sunny morning in Rio de Janeiro with Lisa happily chatting away as usual, little did I realize that this was the day my life would change forever. I recall that morning so very clearly, in my mind's eye, as if I was watching a movie of it.

Nothing I could have done would have prevented the events that lay ahead for my daughter and me that day; I have come to believe to be our fate. Call it destiny if you prefer, perhaps karma, give it whatever term you like, but it was meant to happen the way it happened, and at that precise period in my life.

I know, too, that I was given a warning of these events some months prior to the accident. It was sometime before the Christmas of 1982 when I had the strangest of dreams. As it turned out, the dream was to become an actual living nightmare.

In my dream I saw one of my children falling into a swimming-pool. The child was wearing very little, except for shorts or something similar. When Lisa drowned, due to the hot weather, she was not wearing much.

In the dream, at the place where the child fell into the pool, there were railings very similar to those on our own balcony. Susan's house, too, had an upstairs area with railings and, of course, the swimming-pool in the front garden.

This dream upset me so much that I told another friend, Anna, about it. Now I am very glad I did tell someone before the accident happened, otherwise people may have thought my grief was making me imagine it.

My mother used to say: 'What is for you will not go past you,' meaning that we cannot avoid our fate whatever it may be. My life seemed to lead up to that day, 7th February 1983, and the way it has continued makes me believe that nothing could have stopped the events of that day occurring. Now, through the grace of God, I have been given the help I needed to turn my suffering around and use it for the good of others.

Looking back, although I would have obviously preferred not to have suffered the death of my daughter, I never really thought of Lisa as being mine to keep forever. Even from the first day of her life I had this ominous feeling that I would lose her one day. I had a strong misgiving that I was waiting for something to happen in my life. That one day, somehow, an event was to happen – and it did.

What her death did was to make me look at all aspects of my life before that day. After Lisa's death I began to seek a greater understanding for my own life.

This book tells how I have been able to re-build my life from that dark day of 7th February 1983, to a new life full of hope. I have written it for two main reasons. First, out of fear that Lisa's very existence might be forgotten by others, though never by me or her father. Then, to try to bring to other bereaved parents some measure of hope, however little, and the idea that there are ways forward if they want to seek them, though their way may not be the same as mine.

Tomorrow will come whether we want it or not, and that there are ways of living your life, even a life that feels as if it has no purpose left, as a lasting memorial to a lost son or daughter.

Part One

Mourning a Child

Chapter 1

Early Days

*May my words and my thoughts
be acceptable to you, O Lord,
my refuge and my redeemer!*
Psalm 19:14

The initial reaction to death, any death, is usually disbelief.

If the person who has died is a close family member or friend, shock is also experienced. The intensity of the shock – how and when it is felt, how long it lasts – will vary for different people.

When the loss involves one of their children, the bereaved parents refuse to believe there child is dead. They can see the empty place at the dinner table. They know the child has not been home for a while. Eventually, and it maybe something trivial like a favourite meal being served, reality forces them to accept the unacceptable, that their child cannot come home again.

How do they start to rebuild their lives? Why should they even want to survive this tragic event? Why seek to continue to live without their child?

These are just a few of the questions which run around inside the mind of the bereaved parents, day in, day out. They may drive some to a complete breakdown. Some parents have spent the first few weeks of their loss in a hospital ward, in a state of nervous collapse. This shows how drastically the news can affect them.

Most of them do not wish to go on living, but come to realize that they do not have much choice. What is the alternative? To end their own life would not help to reunite them with their child. To stop the process of living by letting people tend to their needs would only make them a burden for somebody else.

On top of all this, an innate sense of survival is much stronger than their desire to stop living. This means they will survive and life will go on anyway, even when they do not want it.

Following your instincts

My first piece of advice to newly bereaved parents is to trust in their own instincts. Whatever helps them to cope should be used. Each parent is an individual and as such will have to develop their own way of coping. Even the mother and father of the same child may have to find different ways of coming to terms with the loss.

This is a very important concept to grasp. It may help to save your marriage or partnership from dying too. If each is allowed to go forward in their own way, at their own pace, then they are less likely to be intolerant of their partner's way of coping.

Similarly, close relatives may not understand the parents' wishes with regard to the child's funeral. Few parents have had this experience before and in the shock of the circumstances, they will often bow to family custom and tradition. However, most bereaved parents instinctively look for something special and different for their beloved child. If you can convey to your relatives that your wishes, whatever they are, help you to cope, then they will be more able to accept them, even if they disagree at the time.

Many parents, of course, will be so devastated that they will not be able to attend a funeral at all. Staying away should be understood by others not as a slight to the lost child, but rather as the act of a broken-hearted parent.

Getting help and advice

Unless you too are a bereaved parent then you should be careful about how you offer advice to grieving parents, who are very vulnerable. If you are not sure what to say, it is safer not to say anything. Just offer to be with them, allow them to talk, especially about their child.

Yes, it will cause them to cry and perhaps make you cry too, but these are healing tears and should be allowed to flow. Don't be afraid of their tears. They will stop eventually, but they are a very necessary part of the healing process.

On the other hand, not all bereaved parents will cry. Some refuse to allow themselves to do so. This should, again, be tolerated. Don't try to force them into weeping. One day, perhaps, they will do so, or perhaps never. It is the bereaved parent's choice.

There are many ways in which relatives and friends can help. They can support by helping to do the housework, the cooking, or minding other children.

However, none of these should be done without referring to the bereaved parent in the first instance. They still have a mind that is functioning. If they feel they are being treated like sick people, they may become resentful.

This can lead to them over-reacting and saying hurtful things to the person helping. They do not mean to take their anger out on anyone. It's just that some of them will be like volcanoes, with feelings welling up inside which can erupt on to whoever happens to be in the vicinity at the time.

Pain

When the initial shock begins to subside, all that is left is the pain.

The pain endured as bereaved parents is very tangible. It is like no other pain ever experienced before. It cannot be seen by anyone, and this seems odd, because for the suffering parent it surrounds every minute of their life. They have lost a vital part of their body, but no one except them knows how real the loss is.

The pain becomes so much part of a bereaved parent's life that they are loath to let it go. Then they are surprised to reach a point in their grief when their frame of mind begins to change and become lighter. They may be filled with feelings of guilt. 'How dare I allow myself to laugh, let alone smile?' They admonish themselves: 'How dare I feel better when my child no longer lives!'

Letting go of the pain is not always possible. Some parents just cannot let it go. Most of them learn to live with it. They may discover coping strategies which help them to deal with it, mostly though they bury it. The pain is never very far away. It is kept inside and brought out once in a while, indulged in a little, then put away again, sometimes for fear of society's disapproval.

When they have lived with the pain for so long, it can mask all other feelings, even the love they had for the child. No, they have not stopped loving their son or their daughter. It is just that the pain is so strongly connected to the day the child was lost, many feel this is all they have left. At least it is real, while the future is not.

They want to turn back time, but eventually the truth dawns that they cannot. Once they have reached this realization, some will accept, however reluctantly, that they must take those first tiny steps forward, into the future without their.

What society does not realize is that for bereaved parents, it is after several weeks that the early waves of shock begin to lift, and when the real agony truly starts.

From here on, life is an unrelenting pilgrimage through pain and turmoil. For instead of being able to accept what has happened and get on with their lives, they wake up to the reality that their child can no longer be part of that future they are expected to face.

The attitudes of others, of society in general, can cause even more anguish at this stage. It's alright to cry and mourn, so long as the tears are shed in private, and don't make others feel uncomfortable.

Above all, we are expected to 'just get on with it'! But it does not take much thought to see why this is so hard for a parent. When we bring our first newborn baby home from the maternity hospital, we know that henceforth we are responsible for the wellbeing of that child. However much we looked forward to being parents, only at that moment do we encounter the full significance of that obligation.

No one can know when they set out to have children, the cost in emotional terms that this will bring to them. Some of us are natural parents, for others it can be a bit of a shock when at the end of their pregnancy; they suddenly realize they are now responsible for the wellbeing of another human being.

It is not easy to adjust to this third person who is now trying to rule your life and it takes a few weeks and sometimes months to get into a workable routine which suits you, your baby and your partner. Once this has been achieved you can get on with the joy of being a family instead of just a couple.

When we lose a child, then, in whatever way, we are losing the baby we once had. It's as if we are asked to readjust our lives once more to exclude that person. However, we cannot do this shedding overnight. It can take years to work through these emotions because we have to somehow unlearn all that we have learned. Yet, we never truly get over the loss of our child, we learn to live without them in our daily lives, but they are never far from our minds and forever cherished in our hearts.

Shattered hopes and dreams

All of us make plans and have hopes for our children. Even before they emerge from the womb, we have envisaged what they will look like. Usually, we have a boy's and a girl's name already chosen.

If the sex of the unborn baby is known, some parents even put the child's name on to the waiting list of some place of education, because the demand for that particular school is very high.

Some of us will imagine our daughter's wedding day; or dream about our son's selection to play football or some other sport for his country. People never change; neither do our hopes and aspirations for our children.

All these hopes and dreams come crumbling to the ground on the death of a child. All the parents hoped for, all those future scenes of the child's life; vanish in the course of a few minutes or hours of one particular day.

One day the parents may rebuild this world that has collapsed, but they will not be the same people. Their world will never be the same, but if they can hold on to life and be patient, they can make it through to another day, a new day they did not believe was possible.

When that day comes, they will know they have coped in the best way they could in the circumstances, and can smile once again. Then they may look back at that blackest of all days and know that somehow they survived it. They can go on and tell the world of their beautiful daughter or handsome son and be proud to have known them.

Anger and Depression

The many stages in the healing process of bereavement hold different intensities for both the mother and the father of the dead child. This can be due to the type of personality each one has. How we approach our loss can be influenced by our backgrounds. For instance, whether we were encouraged to display emotions as children, openly or not, can have some relevance to the way we respond as adults.

If we are fortunate to have family and friends who are willing to tolerate our moods and listen to our ranting and raving at a time when we no longer seem to be in control of our temper, then perhaps we will be able to grieve in out own manner.

However, many of us, instead of allowing our anger out, will suppress it. Through our childhood we were able to let off steam, but as we grew up we had to learn to control it. When we lose a child, we are caught in a dilemma. We are very angry indeed, but society has taught us not to show this in public. Therefore, in our minds we constantly mull over our hidden feelings.

We may wallow in self-pity and at the same time, probably without realizing it, sink deeper and deeper into depression. Thus we are in a vicious emotional cycle. We become angry, feel depressed, then endure self-pity – and not always in that order. All of these become such a part of our day-to-day life that we can reach a point where they are the only feelings we know.

It is only when we encounter other bereaved parents that we come to understand that, just as happiness and contentment, these negative emotions are just as valid, just as real and equally entitled to be aired. If they are not allowed to come out, then they may be suppressed for a while but will emerge in some form or other, such as in mood swings or skin complaints and for some they may trigger heart disease, or lower resistance to illness.

Then how can we deal with the negative feelings aroused by anger, self-pity and depression? We should admit to them in the first place. This is a major step in starting to heal. Allow yourself to feel them in some measure. Try to recognize whether they are controlling you or you them.

Self-pity is still very frowned upon and many of our society will not tolerate it in any way. Yet, why should we not feel sorry for the situation we have to suffer? Unless other people have had the same sad experience, then they will not understand that we are entitled to feel this emotion.

We can start to turn the self-pity around by being kind to ourselves. Do not expect too much of yourself too soon. If you want to stay in bed all day, do it. If you have other children to tend, see to them, put them out to school or work, then make a thermos of tea and go back to bed and indulge yourself.

Put a TV in your room, so you can use it to 'escape'. Often, if your mind is partly occupied with other people's problems then you will be distracted. No, you won't stop thinking of your own situation, but your mind will have a small measure of peace.

Perhaps, on the other hand, if you feel extremely angry you could put your emotional energy into starting a campaign for awareness of the accident or illness that claimed your child's life. If you feel you need to do something physical, go for a run or a cycle to raise funds for a charity which supports disadvantaged children, do a spring clean even if it's not Spring.

If your feelings seem to be dominating your every waking moment, then you should consider seeking medical advice. Some doctors are much more willing to listen to emotional problems than they were in the past, though many will be too hard-pressed to give the time you feel you need. If you can convince your doctor that you need more than pills to help you, then there may be counselling services in your area to which you can be referred.

If depression were dealt with earlier and given a better response, then bereaved parents would not, as many do, end up becoming permanently low, or even needing long-term psychiatric care.

It is ironic that we have to learn the hard way how to deal with these very strong negative emotions. Furthermore, that we have to find a channel for these feelings to escape, because if we suppress them as we may have brought up to do, they can become very destructive. Then, not only will we have lost our children, we will have been destroyed, too.

Many bereaved parents might say: 'What's the point of living anyway, if my child is dead?' Some might be glad not to rediscover a purpose to their lives.

Yet we might equally ask: 'Will it bring my child back, if I stop living too?' It would be better, surely, to go on fighting through our pain and loss, for our child's sake.

Would it not be a more fitting memorial to a child for us to say: 'I am glad I knew them' and to celebrate having had them sharing our lives? To believe it is better to have loved and lost, than never to have known them at all?

Chapter 2

Going Forward

As bereaved parents reach a stage in their grieving where they understand that they cannot go back, they may be equally afraid of going forward, and so become stuck in a rut. They are not sure what to do for the best. Many feel they are on a roller-coaster, with their emotions going up and down, with moods swinging between guilt, anger, sadness or tears. They may not have experienced such very strong emotions before, arriving all at once or one after another, and may not know how to interpret them or deal with them.

Some may suffer a terrible attack on their self-confidence, and if this was poor before the loss, they may be without the strength or means to help themselves.

Some go into a denial phase. Others are so afraid of admitting to their feelings that they do not allow them to surface for fear of going out of control. For one thing society loathes is a person out of control.

In British society, it is frowned upon to show unhappy emotions, especially in public. Indeed even today, in news bulletins the camera lingers on anyone who may be tearful, because it is still so unusual to see someone cry openly, all the more so if it is a man. Our society expects bereaved parents to adhere to this 'norm' of silent suffering. Nevertheless, we need to let these emotions out, and this is where counselling may be of value. (I discuss this topic at more length in Chapter 4.)

These days there are many help sources for trauma victims and it is widely recognized that counselling in the earliest days can save a lot of anguish later on.

Many people, especially more senior members of society, do not seem to see the need for counselling. They appear to think today's generation has gone soft, asking: 'How is it that we managed to cope with hardships, never mind two world wars, without all this nannying?'

However, these days we live in a very fragmented society, which means the back-up of the extended family no longer exists as strongly as in the past. We have become much more self-reliant, and at a younger age than ever our parents were. This means when troubles arrive, we are more likely to expect by ourselves to know how best to deal with them.

When people lived closer to their family and when families were larger, there was more likely to have been a relative who had lost a child, especially by miscarriage. This would have given people some awareness of how to cope with such tragedies.

In a society where people are no longer so interdependent, we are reluctant to admit we need help. It takes either courage or desperation to make us reach out to someone else. Only when we realize we are drowning in self-pity, or our family and marriage are falling apart, do we look to find some way out of our despondency.

Many bereaved parents have found that as soon after they have made that initial small step into the future, they are genuinely surprised at the relief they feel. Their feelings may still be tinged with guilt, but they begin to see hope arising out of despair, and so are learning gradually to move forward.

Seeking a way forward

Many come to realize sooner or later that, since they are still alive, they have to make the most of life, whether they like the idea or not. Much as they would rather curl up and stop breathing, they cannot. They might have other children. They may have a partner who needs them to be stronger than they are themselves.

There may well be parents who quickly follow their children to the grave. Most of us, however, despite our anguish, will find a need to go on living – whether this is because of a deep-rooted survival instinct or not, I do not know.

We don't want to leave our children behind, but we must go on, somehow, by whatever means we can. Again, I would stress that, as individuals, it is important to be true to ourselves. Other people, especially those who do not know the depths of child loss, may consider our means to be crazy, unnatural or even perverse.

However, does their opinion really matter, when they have no idea whatsoever of the despair we have to endure? This means we have to find an inner strength, which will help us to cope with our loss as well as, on occasion, society's disapproval.

In many instances it is we who find ourselves comforting others, instead of them supporting us. It is our arms that go around others, our voice reassuring them that: 'Yes, it is truly awful, but don't worry. It's just one of those things life throws at us.' Then they will compliment us on how strong we are, not realizing that we are in deep turmoil and resentful that, yet again, the bereaved has become the comforter.

Through these trials, we begin to learn that we can help ourselves to move forward; probably more so than well-intentioned counsellors ever can.

What about my child's possessions?

But how do we start? Where do we start? A first step is often to wonder what to do with our child's bedroom, with their clothes, with their possessions? Shouldn't I keep everything the way it is? Why do I have to be the one to pack up their things for the last time?

Many bereaved parents have problems knowing how best to deal with their child's things, and whether to leave photos on display or put them away in the family album.

What I would suggest is try not to react too hastily. Some parents, in their anger and despair, throw all photos in the bin. However, if you cannot bear to look at photographs of your child, put them away in drawer or somewhere in the child's room. At least, then, you know where they are should you ever want or need to look at them again.

Put it this way: if you lost a parent or grandparent, you probably would not throw their photos away, or store them out of sight. True, it may be not be easy to look at photos of your child, but in time these pictures could help you retain your memories and eventually, even, happy ones will return.

Dealing with a child's personal possessions isn't easy, and depending on the child's age, it presents parents with different problems. Lisa was only three years old when she drowned. Therefore, compared to a teenager, she had much fewer belongings. Yet, to me it was a whole lifetime's worth.

Some parents keep their child's room exactly as it was the last time their son or daughter used it. They cannot bear to have anything removed. Some won't even allow the room to be dusted until it is absolutely essential, and then everything must be put back just as it was before.

Equally, some parents give their child's things to charity or pass them on to other children, or sell them and give the proceeds to a good cause.

Some seek particular ways of remembering. Parents who have lost a school-age child made a collage from their child's artwork and drawings. Others had a tree planted in the child's honour, either in their own garden or in a public park.

Remembering and forgetting

For the memories to be a comfort rather than an anxiety, it is important to find people who are willing to talk with you about your daughter or son. Sometimes friends are more willing than family. I think that our family themselves are sometimes too close to the loss to understand that what we need most of all is to be allowed to remember our children. To be allowed to talk of them freely as if they still lived; because by doing this we are reassured that they did exist and are worth remembering. For the biggest fear is that if other people forget our child, we will be forced into doing this as well. It takes us a while to realize that this will never happen.

How many children do you have?

New friends, that is, friends made after the loss can be very difficult to handle. What do you say when asked how many children you have? You know what you want to say, but you are encouraged to respect other people's sensitivities before your own.

Instead of being clear and open about it, you might mumble the answer, hoping they do not inquire further. Or you may blurt out the number of children you have now and wound yourself with guilt for not declaring the deceased child in the number.

Over the years of supporting bereaved parents, I have been asked many times how they should reply to this question. I am afraid all I can suggest is to play it by ear. If you think the person asking it can handle the truth. Tell them, but then they may wish to know some of the nitty-gritty. Go ahead, if you can deal with it at that moment.

Others, on hearing the truth, might change the subject and pretend they did not hear by ignoring your answer. On the other hand they may even walk away from you, indicating they do not want to know any more details. It is a bit like walking on glass – someone is going to be hurt and it might be you.

I am no different even after several years of being a bereaved parent. I still pause when asked how many children I have. It has only been relatively recently that I have considered us to be a family of six. I do not know why I had not done so before. I had always said a family of five. Nevertheless, counting Lisa, we have actually a family with six members. No, she cannot be with us in body, but most certainly is with us in spirit.

I hope now to be able to declare this when asked the question, in future, as to how many children I have, though I will still weigh up each situation as it arises. As you can see, there are many hurdles and pitfalls blocking the way of bereaved parents in their healing process.

Special Occasions

Bereaved parents often make special plans for the difficult days such as anniversaries. For example, a family I knew would still mark a birthday by having a birthday cake and recalling some pleasant memories of their lost daughter. Some will make a special visit to the graveside on an anniversary to lay fresh flowers on it. These are only a couple of things that parents and families do to remember their precious children who have gone before them.

Then there is Christmas. Again, we can make choices that will help us cope. There is no need to make any special effort to be brave, but if it helps us to get through the day, so be it. This is how I dealt with my early Christmases. I tried to keep busy so that I did not have time to stop and think.

Our first Christmas without Lisa was made doubly difficult because Dave's father died, in the same year, 1983, just six months after his grand-daughter. Not only had we to cope with our inner turmoil, but we needed to help Dave's mother enduring her first Christmas as a widow.

I was quite selfish in my response to her request that we should say special prayers before our Christmas dinner, for both my father-in-law and Lisa. I refused point blank and would not hear of it. To do so would have forced me into the position of having to stop to think about these two severe losses and the deeply painful emotions I knew were just below the surface.

That was our quietest Christmas meal ever. No one wanted to talk. None of us wished to be jolly and festive that year, so apart from things like, 'pass the salt, please' and 'do you want more vegetables?' nothing was said. We had to go through the ritual of opening presents, but this was only really for Kevin's sake.

He was still entitled to his Christmas treats even when we adults were suffering anguish in the process.

Each anniversary became increasingly easier to deal with, though there were still those which caught us unawares, like Lisa's tenth birthday, a time which is always special to a child, or her sixteenth, which is again special in all sorts of ways.

There have been times, too, when my friends' daughters were bridesmaids at weddings where Lisa might have been one as well. These are some of the reasons why we can never get over the loss of our child, as the children they played with demonstrate over and over, the occasions our child might have attended but cannot.

Yes, life does go on, but the pain of the loss goes on too.

A turning point

My main two pieces of advice which are worth repeating, that I give newly bereaved parents are: first, trust your gut instincts. If it seems the right thing do, then do it. Second, take one day at a time – do not look forward until you are ready to do so. As I have said already this decisive moment may arrive sooner that you want. There is no need to go looking for it.

The first support group I attended had been meeting for about six months or so when one of the mothers remarked on how sad our lost children would be if somehow they were able to witness the tears we wept and the sadness we felt.

All of us agreed that we would not like to think that we were causing them anxiety or even unsettling them. We came to the resolution that it was time we began to celebrate the part they had played in our lives, and to try not to be so downhearted about their loss.

This was approximately two and a half years after Lisa's death, and it was about the same length of time for the other parents in the group that day. For us, at any rate, this clearly marked a turning point in our grieving. Yet we were still very far from the completion of our healing process. We could only deal with the present for long time, however, as the weeks turned into months and then into years, gradually we did 'come to terms' with the losses of our children.

The dictionary contains many definitions of the word 'acceptance'. It can mean embracing, affirming as well as understanding. These are logical enough concepts of their own; however, when we receive the news or realize our child has died, the acceptance is the last thing we really want.

We can accept the news at face value, but absorbing it within our hearts and minds is quite different. We know it is a fact that our child will not be home again. Yet our minds play tricks on us. We can often refuse to accept the reality, simply because it is too great a tragedy for us to take in. We go into a kind of self-protective mode of denial.

The process of 'coming to terms' has many stages. These can include guilt, anger and self-pity which in turn can cause bitterness or resentment towards others, and one distant day acceptance.

Each stage needs to be worked through, though not everyone may experience them all, nor go through them in the same sequence. Some might journey through them more easily that others. Most of us are surprised at the degree of intensity with which we experience the extremes of these emotions we have.

We may not experience all of these stages but, if and when we do, there is no set pattern to them. Whatever form your emotions take, it is important to realize that all of them are normal grieving reactions to your loss. Most of us feel them, though not all admit to having them.

Where there is a deep sense of guilt, some parents fear they will be eaten up by it. When anger emerges, couples can tear each other apart verbally as well as physically, by taking it our on each other. As for self-pity, we can and should afford ourselves some measure of it, but we need to keep it under control to some extent, otherwise it can cause us to become bitter, and this is more destructive to ourselves than to anyone else.

Dealing with guilt

One of the biggest dilemmas of close family bereavement is the quandary of the question: 'Why me?' For some reason we assume some responsibility for the death. We seem to need something or somebody to blame, and in most cases, it is ourselves we blame most of all.

We feel somehow that we must have let our son or daughter fall into danger. Did we forget to tell them about the dangers of crossing the road? Did we not remind them to phone us for a lift, if they missed the last bus home? Did we have to argue with them that day? Why did we not make amends before they slammed the door and were gone? Thus we continue to torment ourselves, because if no one else was to blame then it must have been our fault. It stands to reason, does it not?

But guilt can rend us apart. This ominous spectre can haunt us for many years, destroying even the strongest amongst us if we do not learn to deal with it. My own sense of guilt was for not having been more observant and forgetting how unpredictable children can be at the age of just three years old.

I should have been more aware of the danger the swimming-pool presented. Lisa had never gone anywhere near it before, certainly not on her own. Moreover, when she was a babe in arms she had such a fear of water that she hated bath time. Because of this I had decided she should have swimming lessons to dispel her fear. I often wondered if it was the right thing to have done, as gradually she became more at ease in water.

Perhaps, I tell myself, if Lisa had kept her fear of water, she would not have gone near enough to the pool to fall in. Would I still have her today if I had waited until she was older before sending her for lessons? Perhaps this would have been the case, but I do not think the end-result would have come out any differently.

I have discovered as my other children have grown that they can be just as unpredictable at any age. But feeling that there was complacency on my part has made my guilt difficult to deal with.

Although questions and anxieties like these are normal reactions and feelings, we must be careful not to judge ourselves too harshly.

Chapter 3

Finding Help

Bereavement trauma has slowly become more acknowledged as a real problem, especially since the Lockerbie bombing, the Hillsborough tragedy and the Dunblane School shooting. These major disasters have rightly drawn the 'experts' together to study the implications of such events and how to prevent them in the future. So it is very reassuring that, amongst other aspects, the long-term effects of bereavement and the potential psychological damage to some of those affected by the loss of people they love, are now being more recognized.

It should always be remembered that every single child lost is a tragedy to a family. Each loss warrants the same support as is poured out at large-scale disasters, when it will still be the individual families who have to rebuild their lives.

Grief is a very private and personal experience. The sad part of suffering a 'public' tragedy is that the media are more interested in selling newspapers and making the national news bulletins, than in giving the grieving parents time and space to take in what has happened. Instead of respecting that private grief, the reporters rush to jump on the bandwagon of a disaster story.

But the real story is a secret and private one, the traumatic events of the last day of the child's life forever etched on the mind of bereaved parents. Every detail of what they did that morning, everything they said to us that day, what they were wearing the last time we saw them alive, remain in our minds forever.

Self-help groups

Talking to those with the same experience can take us straight to the heart of our problem. In self-help groups there are parents at different stages of their 'journey' – some who have lost children recently, some many years ago, and others at various stages in between. This is why such groups are so valuable. In the group there may be another person at the same stage you are struggling with, and they will be able to say how they are getting through it. They might be able to suggest ways for you to deal with your own struggle because, although our loss is unique to ourselves, we all go through the same grieving process, facing up to its difficulties as they arise.

In addition, since our society is so not keen on dealing with the subject of child death, we need others with the same common bond and similar problems, to share our concerns. This is what leads grieving parents to bereavement agencies such as The Compassionate Friends (TCF), CRUSE who support all bereaved people and SANDS who offer support to parents whose baby is stillborn or dies soon after birth.

These groups are no different from the groups set up for parents and toddlers, or prayer groups, or the numerous groups for special needs children and their carers. They all meet because they have a common need and similar aims and hopes.

Many people who have not needed the support of a group may wonder how a bereaved parent can even desire to pick up the pieces of their shattered life in order to rebuild a new life – of which their child cannot be part. Most bereaved parents will not believe that it is possible to ever consider doing this. However, we do reach a point when we recognize the fact that we cannot go back. Therefore, we must go forward, but how?

We can seek out any of these groups and if they themselves cannot help, they may be able to guide us to the contacts which can best fill our needs. Weeks or months, may pass before we find the group that suits our requirements.

The depressing reality is that most of these groups have very little prominence within society, as a whole. It is not until we need such support that we find out about them. Moreover, many of us only discover them by chance, by hearsay or through someone else having been helped.

Sometimes misguided loyalty on the part of close family or friends can prevent us finding help sooner. Trying to be protective, they may not pass on information received from these groups in case it is too upsetting for us. They do not allow the bereft to make up their own minds on the matter. This can cause resentment later, so it is important to realize that if you are ever offered help for a suffering relative, you should allow them to decide for themselves what they wish to do about it. They may agree with you that they are not interested and do not want or need group support, but at least they will still maintain some control over their own destiny.

Making contact

So how do these groups make themselves known? Many more GPs are now aware of the value of support groups for the bereaved than was previously the case. Doctors' waiting rooms usually have a notice-board with the nearest contact details. Church ministers and priests, too, recognize how supportive bereavement agencies can be and are more willing to suggest them to a grieving parishioner.

In the case of TCF, newly bereaved parents are often contacted in the first instance by a bereaved parent who has read of their loss in the local newspaper and has responded by writing to them, offering sympathy and understanding. Sometimes just knowing others are struggling in the same way as they are, can be enough to offer a glimmer of hope. This might be all a person needs to begin coping with their loss. On the other hand they may be motivated to write back and thus the first link is established.

Mostly, it is the mother who persists in seeking outside support but, thankfully, it is now acknowledged that fathers also need help just as much as mothers do. In our society it is more difficult for men so show their emotions than it is for women. The support they need might be less obvious but they still need to know it is there if they want it.

Whatever support you are offered by an agency or group, the choice remains yours. You will not be pushed of pulled in any direction you do not wish to go. No one is going to instruct you on how best to deal with your grief.

At what stage of their grief parents decide to attend a group meeting varies a great deal. Some need to be part of a group very early in their journey, others months later. It may take a lot of courage, though some will be driven by their desperation for help, to seek out a support group.

Once you have made contact with the organizer of a local group, tell her or him that it will be your first meeting then they will try to arrange to meet you, or have someone else meet you before the meeting, to tell you what will happen at the group. Most will be organized in the same informal manner, but you'll feel better if you have some information beforehand. It is sometimes wise to ask a friend to go with you for your first meeting.

Some people are put off by thinking these groups are very melancholy, but they are not. The groups I have been involved with were never morbid. Yes, we speak of our children and rail at society's attitude towards us. When tears are shed they were welcomed not shunned.

Surprisingly most of the time we spend together is simply that – time with other people whom we can be true to our feelings and yet not experience guilt should we find ourselves laughing through our tears and a silent sense of empathy because we all understand the cost we have paid to become a member of that group.

The Compassionate Friends (TCF)

In the book *Our Children* published by Hodder and Stoughton for TCF, you can read how different parents faced up to their losses, including my own account titled 'Lisa'. The book also explains how TCF grew from its meagre beginnings into a worldwide organization.

Those bereaved parents who first met together in January 1996 in Coventry, never set out to form such an organization. However, they realized how much it helped them and the advantage they gained from supporting each other, and slowly it grew into the organization it is today.

It will continue to grow so long as children die and their parents need help to cope without them. In many families, the deceased are probably only remembered at family gathering such as Christmas, weddings and special birthdays. Outside these events, they are not spoken about and younger members of the family might even forget all about them. The grief of the bereaved parent needs more than this occasional token remembering.

Another reason why we need self-help organizations is because many of us no longer live near to close family members.

We are isolated before the loss and this is greatly intensified by the distance between us and those we need to be near. We value our independence, yet suddenly know the sense of desolation at its most acute level. Why was outside support not required before, for earlier generations, you might wonder? I believe it was always needed – just hard to access, if it was ever available.

At the time that TCF commenced, there was no one group that encompassed all ages of child deaths from a wide variety of causes, and nowhere to go for ongoing support after the initial weeks. As far as I am aware there is still no other support group for grieving parents which addresses child loss from miscarriage to adult, and responds to all causes of death, ranging from natural causes, accident, murder or those affected by suicide. TCF tries to help all involved, from parents to siblings and grandparents, and for as long as they want support. Even parents who have lost children many, many years ago have come forward for support, because at last they feel they have found others who understand and are willing to listen to them.

Each kind of death brings its own difficulties and stresses which are not easily understood by those not in that situation. It takes a tragedy like Dunblane for the general public and politicians to respond with shock and sympathy. But what about the countless number of children killed every year in our towns and cities? We must not forget the many children dying each week in hospitals the length and breadth of this country. Do these tragic stories not warrant an equal response of care and concern, an equal measure of understanding of the individual grief behind them?

Since 1969, TCF has expanded beyond all expectations, not out of choice, I hasten to add, but out of need. In August 1994, I attended the first TCF International Gathering in

Birmingham, England, along with over five hundred parents from many parts of the world.

The involvement of so many nationalities proves just how much TCF is needed and how quickly the movement has spread in just a few years. There are Groups throughout the USA, in Australia, increasingly across Europe and now extends into South and Central America as well as Asia. There is also a group in Israel where parents of all the divisions of that region can come together and mourn the loss of all their children, even if they have perished by means of disharmony and war.

Its aim throughout the world is the same, to support parents who have lost children and who need help from those who have trodden this painful path before them. They need help to find a way forward, to grasp for something to give them hope. Ultimately the loss of a child is the same in any language, in any creed and in any walk of life.

It may surprise many to learn that TCFs' adopted symbol of our children is the butterfly. How can such a beautiful creature represent our children, you might ask? However, etched onto the walls of the concentration camps were drawings of butterflies, left behind by the children who perished in them during the war, a simple symbol to remind us of their existence.

The butterfly is also an internationally recognized symbol of hope. With a lot of love and care our little 'caterpillars' will develop into 'butterflies'. However, the fragility of our children is brought home to us loud and clear with the image of the butterfly. This makes it an ideal symbol of our lost children and is recognized worldwide as such.

Chapter 4

Counselling and Befriending

...In the assembly of all your people, Lord,
I told the good news that you save us.
You know that I will never stop telling it.
I have not kept the news to myself
I have always spoken of
your faithfulness and help.
Psalm 40:9-10

Counselling has for a long time been around in one way or another. It happened in families, only instead of being labelled as 'counselling', it was a chat and a cry if needed, usually with an older female member of the extended family who had time to sit and listen over a cup of tea.

When we experience close personal bereavement for the first time, we are unprepared for the aftershocks which follow because we have not had to deal with the range of emotions caused by such an event.

We discover, sooner or later, that these emotions are part and parcel of deep loss. We are often quite surprised by the way we respond to our loss, especially when we believe ourselves to be unflappable and capable of dealing with whatever life may throw at us. This can have traumatic consequences that can cause us to feel confused and isolated. Some of the effects of our loss can be that we may lose our self-confidence and self-respect, as well as our sense of self-worth.

We have tremendous need of advice, yet quite often we are too embarrassed to ask for it. Then we can find ourselves in an ever-increasing, downward spiral of needing help, knowing we need it, yet refusing to ask for it so as to avoid admitting our weakness.

Society is learning how life's experiences can have such a devastating effect on a person that if they are not given support, a traumatic event can all but ruin their future and have repercussions for their entire family.

There has never been such a wide recognition of counselling as there is now. I sometimes hear folk complain that we are too soft on trauma victims these days. Some feel that people should just get on with living as best the can. 'It will make them stronger if they learn to cope,' seems to be a common sentiment.

The older generation survived war, poverty and hardship, and they tend to say that they came through it all right, so why do young people today need such 'molly-coddling'? What some older folk forget or fail to realize is that many of them did not cope very well at all. What some of them did was to bury painful memories in an attempt to forget about those hard times altogether. As a result some of them have ended their days full of bitterness.

Whether we agree with the need for counselling or not, the reality is that more and more people are seeking it and are benefiting from it.

When do you either seek or offer counselling? This is quite a difficult question to respond to because there is no easy answer. Some people might argue that it should be offered soon after the trauma has taken place. Indeed the police seem to provide it automatically to the victims of some types of crime, such as rape and child abuse. They have come to realize that the best time to unearth the details is as soon as possible after the incident. This is when the victim is most likely to have a clear picture in her or his mind, before the shock of the event takes hold of them, which can result in the victim closing up and either being unwilling or unable to respond efficiently to the police investigations.

However, it is all very well offering counselling, but we need to have respect for the other person's right to say 'no'. Regardless of how we believe they could benefit, the choice is always theirs.

Since many people have moved away from their home towns and families, there is less opportunity to seek advice from older family members who may have experienced some of the 'trials of life'. There is also a considerable need to feel unconstrained by parental guidance. To prove we are adult enough, we want to stand on our own two feet and show the world how mature and strong we are.

When a crisis does occur, then, we are often left feeling very isolated, even though families can quickly rally round at such times. Sooner or later, though, they have to return to their homes which may be many miles away. Then we have to find a way of coping on our own.

The first place we go will usually be to our doctor's surgery, where we are sure we will be given good advice. What the doctor can give us is something to get us through the days ahead, which in most cases will be tranquillizers or anti-depressants. But as the medical profession now realizes more and more, pills can only be a short-term solution, and some doctors will only prescribe tranquillizers as a last resort.

Sadly, GPs do not have the time necessary to devote to patients, who clearly need to talk about their feelings. This is where counselling comes into its own and in many general practices now such services are available on referral, to provide trained personnel who offer us the time to sit and listen whenever we need to talk things through. There are many types of specialist counsellors, some dealing with stress in the family home, others victims of accidents, natural disasters, bereavement and so on.

It is all too easy to denounce those who seek counselling as being weak. Many of us may have thought the same at one time, however, some of us have had a change of heart, once we have realized the benefits to be gained.

My hope is to point out to readers that it does not really matter if other people think it is a weakness to ask for help, no matter the problem. It actually takes a great deal of courage to do just that. It is much easier in the short-term to suffer in silence, but inner suffering can be like a festering sore – unless treated, it can poison our whole life and leave us very embittered.

It does not matter at what stage you decide to seek counselling. It could be you are lucky enough to be offered it soon after your loss. You may not feel you want it in the first few weeks, but that does not bar you from requesting it when you know you need it.

Some bereavement agencies to not provide counselling, instead they befriend parents who have lost their child. The difference between a befriender and a counsellor is a bit vague for some people, but there is really quite a big difference.

Counsellors tend to be professionally trained and taught how to approach and deal with a variety of traumatic matters. Befriending, in the case of TCF at any rate, simply means bereaved parents helping other bereaved parents to learn how to cope with their loss.

They are not professionals though some may have worked as counsellors in their careers, and many bereaved parents may well also need professional counselling to help them. However, the basic aim of TCF is to be there for each other whenever necessary, to 'walk together' as opposed to one leading the other.

It has taken many years to get the message across to professionals, such as doctors and qualified counsellors, that there is a need for a sort of halfway support system provided by people with first-hand experience. Without the need for long specialist training, such people can successfully help others through a rough patch.

If the person giving the support has been through the same kind of trauma, they can be in a better position to help than someone who may only have read the textbook example. It is the same old story – of experience being the best teacher. TCF does now provide some advice and training for bereaved parents who feel they are ready to be a group leader so that they have some resources and ideas on how best to help grieving parents who come to them for support.

Chapter 5

How to Help

A certain degree of animosity can be felt among bereaved parents towards the general public for commonly encountered attitudes from others. This is due mainly to the 'Pull yourself together!' brigade, and the 'Aren't you over it yet?' squad.

We are not whingeing, but we are grieving parents. We need time to heal and time that has no limits. We cannot turn our need for our children off like a tap. Nor can we easily master the mountain of pain that blocks our way forward.

We need your patience, even if we cannot have your understanding. We do not want you to take our place. However, we do want you to stop telling us how to grieve and when it is time to stop – according to your judgement, not ours.

When you first meet a bereaved parent do not feel obliged to say anything. It is often better to say nothing than uttering some trite words that can add insult to injury. Instead hug them, cry with them, or just sit with them. A few minutes are all it will take for them to gain some measure of your concern for them. If you do not know what to do, ask them. They may be remarkably calm initially. It can take a while for the information to penetrate. However, if they are a bit incoherent, just be with them, make yourself available for them.

I was lucky that I had friends who were willing just to sit with me while I retold the 'tragic story' of that awful morning over and over. Each new caller who came to the house, wanted to know how such a beautiful little girl could have been so suddenly taken from us.

The aim of this chapter is to help others to help bereaved parents. What follows is not meant to be confrontational, but a means of breaking down the invisible barriers that prevent people form approaching the already afflicted.

The best way to find our how a bereaved parent is coping, is simply to ask them. If they respond, you can offer to just listen, there and then, to anything they would like to share. If they say 'no', at least you know you have tried. They will appreciate this approach much more than having you tell them that you know what is right for them.

But a very strange thing happens on the loss of our child. People we would have counted as good solid friends unexpectedly evaporate into the thin air. We might have made an effort to get ourselves ready to go out and be pleased we were able to pluck up enough courage to get ourselves out of the front-door. Then we see a familiar face in the crowd, smile in their direction, but they avoid our eyes. Some even cross the road so they do not need to speak to us while others completely ignore us altogether.

Reactions like these and many similar ones happen so often that inevitably we come to realize that people are deliberately avoiding us. Then there are the people who obviously know of our loss, they lower their voices in our presence, yet it is obvious that we are the topic of their discussion.

Because of these attitudes we assume that we are being blamed for our loss, and all our feelings of guilt and helplessness well up to overwhelm us all over again. The sad result of this behaviour is that we believe we would be given more time to recover and more support from others had we lost a limb instead of our child.

After Lisa's accident, I did not have the first idea of how I was going to cope. There was no plan. How could I possibly look towards a future without Lisa to share it? How was I to pick up the pieces and try to rebuild my life when there was such a vital element missing? I was totally unaware of my ability to survive this loss. What I did know and demanded was to have the right to do whatever I had to in order to survive it; fittingly or otherwise, but in my own way. If I was to survive I had to do so using anything and everything I could, just to make the coping that bit more manageable for myself.

This may sound selfish, but sometimes you need to be a bit selfish in such a situation, otherwise you may find other people imposing their methods of coping on you. For some this may be helpful and acceptable, and for those whom it helps, I am very glad, so long as it is what the bereaved person wants. Sometimes there is no other way. Different ways may be just as painful, but they can also be very rewarding.

While I accept most people had my best interests at heart, they were not me and thus they did not know how my mind worked. As an individual I had my own needs, which did not necessarily coincide with theirs.

Bereaved parent may talk of aspects of their loss which sound odd, but it will be logical to them. In effect what they are doing, much of the time, is thinking out loud. They do not need a verbal response from you; just a reassuring nod now and again will be fine. Even if you do not understand why they seem to be talking in circles, there being another person present confirms to them that they are still part of the real world, and helps them hold on to their sanity.

The people, who tried to advise me, in the early days of my loss, suggested I should speak to a counsellor who lived locally, and who would be quite willing to listen to me if I phone her. To the credit of the counsellor, she never forced herself upon me, conveying through another person that she would come to me only if I approached her, and I respected her greatly for this.

Despite telling these people over and over that I did not wish to speak with this lady, they would not listen until I became quite angry and demanded to be allowed to handle my grief my own way.

My way of coping was to turn everything over to God. In effect, He became my Counsellor. I handed over my pain, my despair, my tears and my daughter. In return I asked from Him the means to survive and the desire to do so. Later (see Chapter 9), I tell how He answered my prayers and completely restored my life.

One of the strongest emotions I experienced at the sudden loss was an overwhelming sense of isolation. When our immediate family, for example, does not wish to discuss our child's life with us, we start to imagine that we are alone in grieving for our child, and are left feeling that the rest of our family do not really care about us.

What I have come to understand is that, in reality, our families think that to speak of the dead child will be too painful for us to bear, and we will all end up crying again. However what hurts us more is the invisible wall of silence that goes up between us and those who knew our child almost as well as we did, whenever our child's name is mentioned.

It is often because of their family's apparent inaction that bereaved parents are driven deeper into despair. They have all those memories buzzing around inside their minds, tormenting them, not allowing them to rest. Yet they may have no one who is willing to listen, to help reaffirm their child's life. They need the reassurance that the good memories will not be buried with their son or daughter.

Ask grieving parents how they feel about discussing their child, and they will know at least you have made an attempt to support them. If in the conversation they become sad, angry, and tearful or even laugh at amusing memories, do not hold yourself responsible for the onrush of feelings, as the bereaved parent will have appreciated you taking the time to listen to them about their child.

They may very well laugh one minute and dissolve into tears seconds later, but do not be alarmed. Do not feel you have done anything wrong. Just give them a hug, stay with them, and cry together if it helps. When the tears stop, you will both feel a bit better for having wept.

Many bereaved parents feel that they are in a dark tunnel, not physically, of course, but mentally and emotionally. They seem to be travelling along a road filled with 'landmines' and other hidden obstacles, on a journey the do not wish to be taking. However, somehow they need to go on. They must try to make sense out of a life which has changed in such a drastic way that they feel completely and utterly helpless.

PART TWO

MY OWN JOURNEY

CHAPTER 6

Family and Friends

At the time of Lisa's accident we had been living in Rio de Janeiro, Brazil. We were there because my husband, Dave, worked in the oil industry. We had made many good friends while we were there, both within the company and among local people – Brazilians as well as other foreign nationals.

Since we had a very active bunch of friends, most of them knew Lisa and were horrified by her death. They were all tremendously supportive in those early days of our loss, rallying around and doing what they could to help.

Our Brazilian friends especially took her death personally because it had happened in their country. They adore children and really value them as people in their own right. There, children are the life and soul of their families and welcomed wherever they go.

Our friends kept us going that awful day. There was always one or two around to sit with us, to listen to my never-ending prattle. Also to see to Kevin, I suppose, since I was of little use to him that day.

One family of friends stayed well into the evening, until we managed to convince them that we would be alright, left by ourselves. We did not really know how we would get through that night, but we knew we had to somehow, if only for Kevin's sake.

On the night of the accident someone mentioned something about arranging a Church service on our behalf. Dave and I had agreed that we would like to do this. In the morning much to our surprise, we were awakened by the phone ringing. We were very surprised to have slept at all, because we never imagined we would be able to. On waking we were flooded by tremendous guilt at having slept. How could we have possibly stopped thinking of our Lisa, even in the realms of sleep?

Dave went through to answer the persistently ringing phone. It was one of our friends telling us they had arranged a Church service for that morning. If we did not feel up to driving, they would be along to take us there. When Dave came back to the bedroom to tell me this, the last thing I wanted was to face the day. When he explained that our friends would drive us to the service, we agreed that we might gain some comfort from going. So, reluctantly we dressed and waited for the car to fetch us.

The friends who came were Steve and Hilary Roberts. I knew them to be committed Christians, members of the Pentecostal Church, while Dave and I attended the Catholic Church. I assumed that, whatever service they had managed to arrange at such short notice, it would be in their church. We were in no fit state to care where it was.

How my heart lifted when instead of heading for Steve and Hilary's church they took the direction which led to ours. While I had imagined that we would be going to the service on our own along with Steve and Hilary, there standing waiting for us were many of the staff from Dave's office, and as many of our friends as they could gather. Instead of a short prayer service, which we had assumed would take place; a Mass was said for us and Lisa.

I can never thank those friends enough for what they did for us that first morning without Lisa. Being thousands of miles away from our family, going through hell and not knowing if we could survive, they gave us the first sign that we were not suffering alone.

They did not know how to help us, but there they were, pouring out their love and their tears for us, that bright sunny Tuesday morning. They continued t support us when we eventually returned from Lisa's funeral in Scotland.

My family were really terrific. My brother Raymond acted as liaison with Dave's employers regarding the flight details. There were formalities to be gone through before we were allowed to leave Brazil, but thankfully friends and colleagues rallied round. As Raymond himself is a father, it must have been a very tough task to carry out. Dave and I will always be grateful for the way he handled the arrangements for Lisa's funeral.

We had made the decision to take Lisa home to have her buried in our home city of Glasgow, in Scotland. We had hoped to fly out the same night of the accident, but the paperwork could not be completed in time. Initially, I was disappointed, but it was better to have our first night in Brazil without Lisa, and start to absorb it as much as we could before having to deal with the inevitable questions waiting for us on the other side of the Atlantic.

I do not remember going to, or arriving at, Rio de Janeiro airport, the morning of the 8th February, the day after the accident. I do remember being on the plane and the numerous offers of food from the stewardesses. All I knew for sure was that we were heading home on what was the worst journey of our lives.

At Heathrow airport, we were met by friends we had made in Brazil, but who were now living in London. It was good to see a friendly face in the crowd, people who knew the heavy burden we were carrying.

The final flight home to Glasgow seemed eternal. On the one hand I wanted it to be over, on the other I did not because then I would have to face my family and try to explain somehow how Lisa came to be dead and here we were home to bury her.

We finally touched down at Glasgow airport some time on the evening of the Tuesday. It was a very agonising walk from the plane to the terminal building, but at last I was in the arms of my family.

My worries proved groundless as all they wanted to do on seeing us was to throw their arms around us and pour out all sorts of emotions and tears, but also love – love that I never knew they had for me until then. What a pity that love, so often goes undetected until such moments.

Bereaved parents often have difficulty in getting understanding from immediate family. Perhaps it is because of their love for us that they sometimes cannot stay around and witness the pain they know we are experiencing, because the pain is also unbearable for them.

What our family affords us, above all, is a safe place where we can vent the anger brewing up inside us. If we rant and rave at friends we might lose them for good. With our family, we can often let rip and still know, or at least hope, we can make it up to them, when we are more able to cope.

As we had been in Rio for two and a half years when Lisa died, we were offered two options. We did not have to return to Rio after her funeral. We could choose to stay in Scotland and all our belongings would be packed up and shipped home to us. We could return and finish our time there and be relocated in the usual manner, as generally the company moved its employees after about three years, sometimes back to Britain or on to another foreign posting.

We opted to go back to Brazil and finish our time there. There was an understanding that if living there proved too difficult for us, then the company would allow us to go home to Scotland and Dave would be given a position in their Aberdeen office.

We had been doing pretty well under the circumstances, or so I believed. We had been through a very rough time, but from the day of our return in early April 1983, we started to make slow yet steady progress, learning to take one day at a time.

Our loss happened in Brazil, but it could have befallen us wherever we happened to be living, The place is not important – though the remoteness from family may have had some bearing on the methods we chose to cope. Because of the distance, it was impossible for me to have my mother stay with me.

Nor were we able to pick up the phone whenever we were feeling low and in need of family comfort. This made me realize very quickly that we had to do whatever we could to get through each new day; Dave and I had to find our own way of doing this.

Although my life had abruptly altered there was a real need in me to get out and about. I realized quite soon after the accident that I would have to try to do positive things to help myself cope. I am by nature a practical person and I believed no good would come from sitting around moping.

For one thing Kevin still had his life ahead of him. For his sake, as well as my own sanity, I had to get out of our apartment. I had to circulate and let people know I needed company, not isolation. I had to do something, go somewhere to get out of our apartment, and away from the deafening silence within it.

I was lucky that most of the people I phoned were delighted to hear from me and understood my need for companionship. I began by taking Kevin back to his toddler group. Even on the first occasion back, it was obvious he really enjoyed having the freedom to play with other children. At the tender age of fourteen months, he had really only just begun to interact with Lisa when he lost her.

I am afraid I was probably too wrapped up in my own pain to attempt to understand how much Kevin must have missed his big sister. There was a big gap in his little life and he did not know what it was. If he did, he did not have the means to tell us, even if we had been in a frame of mind to listen.

Going back to my familiar routine resulted in confused emotional reactions. On the one hand I desperately needed the company and the distraction gained by my weekly sessions of Mah Jjong and Bridge lessons. On the other hand, it took every ounce of my strength to get through each session. Whenever I eventually arrived back at our apartment, I would collapse in a heap on the sofa and more often than not, weep copious tears.

To others it must have seemed that, rather than living every pain-filled moment of my grief, I was denying my loss, and comments started to be made. One person in particular, badly affected by Lisa's death, became worried about me and my behaviour, and she found it difficult to understand how I could even leave the house so soon after losing my child. She thought I was going mad because she could not understand why I needed to go back to my social routine. All she had to do was ask. It would have been far better if she had been open and honest about her concerns.

I had enough problems trying to deal with my own grief without trying to defend my actions and without other people enforcing their suggestions upon me. This made me not only angry, but displeased as well as disappointed at being pushed in a direction I believed would have been wrong for me. If I was going to survive this greatest tragedy of my life, I had to do it my own way and not necessarily in a conventional manner.

Eventually I came to feel that I would be continually watched and my behaviour commented on if we stayed in Rio, so I asked Dave to find out if the offer to ship us home was still available. Thank goodness it was. So we set about the business of packing up our belongings and heading for Aberdeen and the familiar surroundings of Scotland.

We still would not be very near to our families, who lived in Glasgow, but we would be in the same country as them, within four hours' drive, and they would be able to give us comfort if we sought it.

Once we were back in Scotland, I knew immediately we had made the right decision. My spirit was lifted be the mere fact that I was home. Now what I had to do was convince the world and those friends in Rio whom I had left behind, that I was not running away from reality. I was simply trying to come to terms with my loss, in my own way, in my own time and in my home country.

CHAPTER 7

My Way, My Choices

I cried you for help, O Lord my God,
and you healed me;
You kept me from the grave.
I was on my way to the depths below,
but you restored my life.
Psalm 30:2-3

When Lisa died there was little help available to bereaved parents. Lacking guidance, I did what I did because it felt right at the time. I suppose this has been my yardstick all along. Unless I felt strong enough or had a reasonably good instinct about what I was about to tackle – be it Lisa's toys or clothes or whatever – then I would postpone it until I was ready to deal with it.

It was about eight or nine weeks after Lisa's death that I asked my friends to help me sort out her room. I did not tackle it all on the same day though. I was not that brave. Her clothes were the first items to be sorted, and then a few days later, perhaps a week or more, we dealt with her toys.

For me this had to be done early on in my grieving. I am not sure why, but I knew it had to be done one day and I much preferred to get on and do it, rather than worry over it, knowing it still had to be done.

Probably knowing Lisa's belongings would be welcomed where they were going helped me get some perspective on the practicality of the task. It was far better if the clothes and toys were being used by other children than hanging in a wardrobe of lying in a cupboard unused.

I had no qualms about going into Lisa's bedroom. Each time I went in, I felt a very calming sensation. Whenever I was feeling a bit uptight, I would go into her room, sit down for a while and contemplate her loss. I would come out feeling much better and more relaxed.

Although Lisa was only three when we lost her, she had acquired quite a few possessions in those few short years. Having friends who were willing to help me sort through her things made the task easier. Though I had definite places in mind where I wanted the various items to go, I did not have to carry out those tasks myself.

For instance, Lisa's clothes went to a friend who found it hard to make ends meet and who had three young daughters of her own. Lisa's girl toys and some of her others, were sent to a children's school where I knew they would be put to good use. Her toddler T-shirts and shorts which were suitable for a boy, I kept for Kevin.

I also used her plastic cups and plates fro Kevin. It was not easy and I wondered sometimes if it was the right thing to do, but in the normal scheme of things that is what would have happened if I had still had Lisa. Her little brother would use her plastic utensils when she had grown out of needing them.

I discovered that because I used Lisa' things it helped me to hold on to her a bit longer. Indeed some of her toddler games and jigsaw puzzles have been played with by my three other children.

Far from causing tears they gave me opportunities to introduce Lisa to Marc and Fiona who, of course, never met their sister. However, I believe that they have a right to know of her and when they have wanted to know more about her, I have been happy to tell them. I know that, by playing with some of Lisa's toys, they can comprehend better that she was a real person and not just the girl in the various photographs spread around our home.

Moving on

The paradox of 'moving on' is strange. On the one hand I realized I was making progress with my grief, and then I would panic – surely if I was beginning to feel better, was I not being disloyal to Lisa's memory?

However, when given reassurance from other bereaved parents that these are 'normal' responses to have, we begin to realize that the process of 'moving on' can be very slow. We still have intense pain, but we are progressing nonetheless.

Although our mood lifts, this does not mean we are forgetting our children, but getting used to them not being around any more. We shan't ever forget them, and we will always miss them and want them back, because the love we have for our children lives on and will never die.

When we reach this stage, which may not be on the same time-scale as any one else, we may be able to begin to celebrate the live our children had, however brief they were.

In saying this, I am mindful that, in the case of babies who die before they are born or soon after birth, their parents have not been afforded this time. I have heard at least one parent in this situation say that she felt the loss would have been harder for her to cope with had her baby lived longer. Difficult as it was, she was sure that she would have found my situation harder to bear, the loss of a toddler.

This is not to say that any loss is less tragic than another. It is more to do with the different 'straws' we grasp at when we are in difficult situations. These may sound trivial in comparison to our children's lives, but it is what some of us have to do to survive. We need to be aware that somehow, someone has found it more difficult than we have, and yet come through their trauma, somehow. In this way we might be able to avoid becoming so wrapped up in our own problem that we become bogged down in self-pity and drown beneath it.

I believe the whole grieving process – though others prefer to call it the healing process – is a journey fraught with choices. Each time we come to an occasion such as an anniversary or birthday, especially within the first year of our loss it has to be dealt with by some means. Again, we have a choice about how we, personally, are going to deal with it. A number of us will do nothing but worry about it and as the day approaches become more and more anxious. Then on the day itself, find it was not as bad as we had imagined it would be.

Important choices have to be made about our family, too, whether or not to have more children, and then how to deal with our anxieties as they begin to grow. I gained enough courage to have two more children, Marc and Fiona, a brother and sister for Kevin. I have been able to allow them space to grow, although it has not been easy at times. To let them go from my supervision, for example, to scout camp, to stay over at friends' houses, and basically to have a normal childhood. That little voice of anxiety and doubt often nagged at me – but thankfully I managed to ignore it, and they have each grown into three nice, decent people.

The need to talk

Can good ever come from a tragedy such as the death of a child? For me, at any rate, I had to make good come out of Lisa's loss, if only to be selfish in reminding people of my little daughter, just in case they were beginning to forget her.

What really made me decide to do something in remembrance of her was that a good few years before my loss one of my aunts lost her son, David, when he was about three years old. I think I was about eleven or twelve at the time. He was a really beautiful little boy and he brought a ray of sunshine to our whole extended family. However, while he was our playing on his tricycle he was run over by a truck.

Knowing of this event in my family's history gave me a bit of hope; because here was someone I knew personally who had gone through the same hell as I was going through. Perhaps, she might be able to help me. However, I never got the chance to ask her. I happened to mention my hope to another aunt, and she seemed horrified that I could even dream of talking about David's death. She shook her head saying adamantly: 'Oh! We do not talk about that anymore!' They were making it quite clear that no one would thank me for raking up the past – least of all the aunt who had lost her son.

Thus, I was promptly silenced and I never did pluck up the courage to speak about that common bond we had. Some years later, we spoke around it but not about it.

From then on I made the conscious effort to continue to talk openly about Lisa. It is significant that with close friends and strangers, I could talk about her more easily than with members of my own family. Now, however, when Lisa's name crops up in conversation at home with our other children, it happens very naturally in the course of our discussions, and not just for the sake of it.

There were times when, for various reasons, I did not have opportunities to talk about Lisa and I noticed on these occasions my mood would change. Though I believed I had been coping well enough, I would unexpectedly become angry and depressed. I came to understand that this was the direct result of not being able to talk about her; not necessarily about her death, but primarily of the times she shared with me. This is when I realized the real worth of bereavement groups meeting regularly. While it might not have been the desire for everyone to talk about their child, it gave each of us the opportunity to do so if we wanted. No one forced us to talk, nor did they try to stop us when we did.

Yet we each gained from hearing the others stories finding common ground and thus attempting to make sense of our situations and yes, striving towards a point when we could, perhaps, answer the 'why me?' question; though this can never be truly comprehended by most of us.

By meeting with other bereaved parents, I have met many wonderful people who have suffered much more as a result of their tragedies than I have. For instance, I cannot begin to know the pain of losing a baby at birth; though I have suffered three miscarriages. I have not known the grief experienced when parents lose their only child. I cannot imagine the hurt felt by older parents who lose an adult son or daughter. Nor that pain endured by parents whose children have taken their own lives or that of murdered childrens' parents. I do know the pain of losing a little girl who had just cast off her babyhood. I do not dare to contemplate losing another child, for I believe that would destroy me totally.

These are all just examples of the severity of loss which some parents are living with. There are many, many more causes of child loss. All are different, but each group of parents can help each other, because we all understand what it is to loss our own child.

We all tackle our losses differently because our children were all different. This is why we each have to search to find our own way to deal with it. Some of us will deal with it better than others. Moreover, this is why we have to respect each other's choices and each other's needs, and hope they will have the same respect for us.

In our grieving, as in many other aspects of our lives, we should be allowed to be adaptable. We should be able to yield to meet the needs of those around us who require a different approach. We are not carbon copies of each other, not are our emotions identical or the ways in which we face up to trauma. Over the many years of providing support to bereaved parents, I have come to learn there are many different ways we can learn to cope.

Most of us do not want to go on living without our child, but most of the parents who come to TCF at least want to try to do so; not necessarily for themselves, but more for their surviving children. They have acknowledged that they need some kind of help from someone who really does understand how they feel and what they are going through.

CHAPTER 8

Finding my Way Forward

I understand why many bereaved parents lose their faith, even a strongly held faith, as a result of their child's death. I know how angry I became with my own situation. I needed to know why I had to suffer in such a dramatic and tragic way. Once I was confronted by a very angry mother who had lost her adult daughter. She was demanding to know why I did not blame God for my loss. She stunned me with her hostility.

All I could say was that I did not blame God. However, I could not have begun to explain to her my inner feelings on this matter, because at that time I was still working through them myself. I had not reached the stage of my journey through my grief where I could intentionally vent my anger, verbally or otherwise.

No, I did not blame God for Lisa's death, but several years later my anger finally surfaced when an acquaintance lost her baby soon after he was born. I was shocked by the intensity of my reaction on the day that I learned of her loss. Perhaps I had not realized it was there lying dormant waiting to erupt. It did within the confines of my own home and thankfully there was no one to witness it otherwise they may have thought I really had gone insane. I do not think I was denying my anger; I just had not been ready to deal with it until then.

My way of dealing with my loss is not unique. It has many similarities to the way other bereaved parents cope. The way I did manage to cope is the only way I could have done so. I did experience guilt and uncertainty by choosing a different way from what I believed was expected of me, but it was no use trying to live a lie. We have to be true to ourselves no matter the circumstances.

Many people tried to influence my decision. Some friends thought I dwelt upon Lisa's loss for far too long. At that moment in time I thought this as well. However, something keeps me striving for more improved support for people who are badly affected by a death in their family, especially that of their child.

Often I have believed that it was time to move on and let someone else do it. Time and again I have tried to walk away, turn my back and stop giving my support, or thought of not answering another call to support yet another grieving mother or father and hoping somebody else will come to their aid instead of me.

When I first made contact with TCF, I was shocked to learn that the principal contact for the whole of Scotland was one person, the late Mary Flannigan, in Glasgow. She, along with a few other parents, was trying to support grieving parents over a huge area.

When I discovered the extent of the task they were undertaking, I felt compelled to write to Mary offering whatever help I could. If she wished, I would be the contact for the Aberdeen area.

My offer was gladly accepted. This was the start of our regular correspondence (which was to last until her sad death just a few years later). From her letters I came to know her as a woman with great strength and fortitude.

Once I had assured Mary that I was willing and capable of helping within my area, she began to send me letters from bereaved parents living near me and throughout the Aberdeenshire area. Gradually my name became familiar to many bereaved parents and care agencies. Eventually, I became the County Contact for TCF Aberdeen and Aberdeenshire.

Most nights I would receive a phone call from someone needing help, or rise in the morning to find another letter on the doormat asking for leaflets or asking to be referred to someone in similar circumstances to the letter writer. Hardly a day went past when I was not contacted by somebody needing TCF support.

Slowly, my network of grieving parents grew. Then we formed a house group where we met once a month in someone's home, to talk over thoughts and feelings which were troubling us or which we had difficulty in resolving.

Every few months, it seemed our numbers grew, but still we met resistance from the professional bodies surrounding us, doctors, ministers and health agencies. They seemed to think we were trying to tell them how to do their jobs.

All we were doing was trying to show them the way we wanted to be treated – to be given time to talk, not pills and potions, then left to get on with it, sink or swim.

To me the real significance of TCF and other such organizations, is that it does not claim to be anything other than a befriending network, It does have to adopt some profession methods for approaching people in need. However, by becoming too professional it could alienate those who, for whatever reason, are not seeking professional assistance, but still requiring help.

In saying this, since bereavement can have really deep-seated effects on some people, TCF members may need to learn to recognize when a person needs a more professional form of support. Members may feel they are able to take up training in counselling techniques, bearing always in mind that we are 'walking together' along the road of grief. Indeed TCF now gives training for those bereaved parents who wish to be the main contact for new members and those newly bereaved.

It is true that not all bereaved parents will need or desire the sort of support that self-help agencies provide. However, the task of letting newly bereaved parents know of their existence is still quite difficult to achieve.

Well-intentioned family members often refuse to pass on letters or messages relayed to them from bereavement agencies. It is true that mistakes have been made in the past when an approach has not been required. Self-help groups have learned a lot over the years. While it is impossible to rule out errors of judgement in the future, there is never an intention to harm, only to offer help, then allow the bereaved parents to decide for themselves if they wish to follow up with the contact information they have been given.

Finding a reason

That it may be possible to find a reason for a child's death is an idea that some can comprehend and that others refuse to accept. A lot of parents may not want to be given a reason or even seek one. This is alright, too. Whatever your own conclusion, finding a reason is still not an easy thing to do.

I believe I am entitled to the right to accept my own understanding of why Lisa was born only to die little more than three years later. If this is what I believe or choose to believe, then all I ask is that others respect my reasoning and do not judge me. In the same way as I will give them respect without judging.

What I am about to write in the next chapter, may in many people's view be extremely hard to comprehend, let alone accept. Nevertheless, it is the point where my journey through my grief both starts and ends. Read what I have to say with compassion. Do not condemn me simply because it is hard to get your head and heart to understand my words. Try not to be offended by them and certainly do not take them personally. They are my own views, my own discernment, and above all my acceptance, mine alone.

CHAPTER 9

My Counsellor

I waited patiently for the Lord's help;
then he listened to me and heard my cry.
He pulled me out of a dangerous pit,
out of the deadly quicksand.
He set me safely on a rock and made me secure.
He taught me to sing a new song,
a song of praise to our God.
Psalm 40:1-3

In saying that my personal Counsellor was and is God or, if you prefer His Spirit, I know I am risking being labelled as arrogant to claim the right to make such an assertion.

Many may ask, what makes me so certain about this? I know it because I have been living with this belief ever since the day I lost my daughter. For when I believed I was going to lose her I prayed desperately that God would give me the strength to survive this tragedy happening right before my eyes. I did not need doctors to tell me she was dead. Call it mother's instinct or feminine intuition, but I knew in my heart that Lisa could not be resuscitated, and thus she was gone.

Whenever I look back to that awful day, I remember it as if it were a movie, but played in slow motion. It must have all taken place within minutes, but at the time living through those last moments of Lisa's life; it seemed a great deal longer. Such a lot happened: getting her out of the swimming-pool; my friend yelling at me to phone for help while she tried to bring Lisa back to life; remembering about the medical centre just around the corner from the house, and running there with Lisa, in the hope they could do something to save her.

While all this was going on, in the middle of it all I had time to pray. I suppose like many people in a moment of crisis, I prayed. I tried the one last thing we are told everyone does at the point of someone's death. I turned to God in desperation. I prayed that Lisa would be alright and that she would survive.

When I realized it was unlikely that she would, I prayed then for the strength I would need to cope without her. Even then I knew I would not be able to deal with this situation without God's saving grace.

Many people might assume that I have always been a strong believer. This was the case for a long time. Particularly in my childhood I truly believed in the power of God. However, like many of us, my faith dwindled during my teenage years. Then I began to question the evilness in the world and questioned why so much suffering was 'allowed' to happen, especially, when I lived in a poverty stricken country like Brazil and saw so much deprivation wherever I looked. (Thankfully now the Brazilian economy has become much better in recent times they may have begun to address some of the problems I witnessed when I lived there.)

Before Lisa's accident, I had come to doubt that God even existed. I stopped attending church and I even read all sorts of distasteful books during this rebellious phase, of a kind which I would never normally have had in my house let alone be reading. I had almost become a complete atheist.

Then a girlfriend, who has a very strong Christian belief, gave me a small book to read which offered answers to a lot of questions I needed answered. This thought provoking book provided me, clearly and in simple layman terms, with the answers I needed. This was my first step back towards my recommitment to God, and a new, profoundly rooted faith in Him.

It was while driving to Susan's place with Lisa, the morning of the tragedy that I fully accepted God back into my life. Within an hour or two my daughter had drowned. Yet I could not walk away from this new-found faith which I had just discovered. Thanks to the Lord, I did not because as I stated before, it has indeed been a truly saving grace.

This was the reason that, when friends were suggesting I should seek counselling for myself, I refused, mainly because I believed that my help would come directly from God. He would give me the help I needed. I had no doubts that He would be true to my convictions, and He has been. I did not tell my friends this because I was quite sure they would not have believed me or understood.

As I did not tell them, this may have been why some of them reacted in the way they did. They believed I would benefit from counselling and possibly by my not allowing them to provide this for me, it made them feel unappreciated. This was not my intention, but how could I get across to these people that I knew God would provide for my needs. They might have been even more convinced that I was becoming unstable because of my grief.

At that time I did not have the fortitude to explain all this to others. It was not a risk I felt I could afford to take. I knew I had to put my trust in God to help me, and to allow Him to guide me through somehow. Of course, I did not know how He would do this, but He did and still does.

First, I had to hand over my loss and my pain to Him; then I had to learn to listen to Him, and hear what He wanted me to do. The hardest lesson I had to learn was to be patient. He wanted to help me, but the timing had to be right.

I do not claim that my grieving was plain sailing after that night, far from it. I had no idea how long and difficult the road through my grieving would be. I failed to appreciate and did not realize that although my faith became my strength, as a human being I still had human weaknesses. I also needed somewhere where I could go to talk about my ordeal. Moreover, I had to learn to accept what had happened, which meant persisting throughout with the pain, the isolation and the despair. On the one hand I could cope and was able to use my loss for other people's benefit, but I simply did not realize how long and slow my own healing process would be.

When my daughter drowned I had little prior knowledge of similar tragedies, yet the very day she died I was almost inundated with information about such tragedies from visitors who came to see us that day. It was because of my incessant need for answers that I never stopped searching for a reason for Lisa's death, but I had to find out, also: 'What was the reason for her life?'

One reason I have considered and with which I find a degree of acceptance with, is that Lisa had a mission in life; and this mission was to show me a route to God which I would not have found by myself. Her life and death brought an understanding to me of the Word of God which Jesus taught through the Gospels.

I believe this because the searching I did after her loss made me examine everything to do with my own life, my place in the world, my own parents and childhood and the effects on my ability to cope with the situation that I found myself in.

Without the tragedy of Lisa's death, my life would have followed a different path from the one I took. I might not have had the strength to go on and have two more children. Had Lisa lived; my life may have been wrapped up in nursing her. I realize she may have made a full recovery, though I do not believe she would have done. Yes, of course, I wish I had been able to keep her and have my other children, but that was not to be.

I believe I accepted the way that God had set for me. He knows me better than I know myself. He knew the way I would go before I did. He has led me all the way, though sometimes I have stubbornly resisted His directions. Even though I have wavered and doubted my own strength of faith and ability, He has not, and He has waited patiently for me to follow Him.

If Lisa had not died, then my life would have carried on as usual, wanting to draw closer to God, but not really feeling adequate enough to do so. I believe if she had not been born at all, I would have carried on with no firm belief in God or Christianity. However, since she did share my life and subsequently she died, these two components added together helped to cast me into a realm of which I would still be unaware had she not live at all.

I know the path I chose in dealing with Lisa's loss was full of questions. I needed to question everything in my life, past and present, not only when I had to suffer the loss of my daughter. I was compelled to find an answer to this and I kept probing until I found out what I needed to know. I did find many; if not all the answers I sought.

Nonetheless many of these answers were hard to accept and others radically altered my view on a lot of aspects of my life. I have to admit that many times I was close to the abyss, because the answers I found were, to me, mind-blowing. I have accepted them, but not before much anxiety and soul-searching. The replies I received made clear to me the breathtaking power of the Will of God and that 'His Will' shall be done whether we like it or not.

So where was my free will, you might wonder? Well, each new step I took forward was down to my choice. As I insisted on going my own way, much of my journey appeared to be very slow. I always hesitated before moving on. I would compare 'traditional' ways with the alternatives, sometimes opting for the former at times.

The biggest gain I have received is the knowledge of God's abiding faith in me. Even when I did not want to listen He never gave up on me. He held me true to the path He had mapped out for me. He never pushed or pulled, but waited patiently for me to turn back to the path each time, as He knew I would, eventually.

CHAPTER 10

On Reflection

There is no right or wrong way to grieve for a lost child. There is only our way – that is whatever we consider right for us as individuals. Yes, we may do things or react in ways other people think are unsound. At the end of the day, it is we who are going through it, not them.

We should learn to be kinder to ourselves. In our protracted grieving, we can only act on the here and now. We will drive ourselves demented by constantly looking forward and trying to second guess how our decisions will pan out, wondering if we should do this or that. We should try to take one day at a time, one step at a time.

Tomorrow will come whether we like it or not, but if we can find enough hope to take us through today, then that will be adequate to get us through the rest of the healing process step by step.

It is not easy to recognize when the clouds are beginning to lift. It can even be a very confusing situation when this stage is reached, because many of us are reluctant to let go of the pain for fear of being disloyal to our child. Although the pain is frequently overpowering, at least it is tangible, something to make us aware of our loss. We are afraid that in letting go of the pain we lose a vital link in the chain that invisibly helps us hold onto our child.

When we reach the stage when our mood begins to lighten, we can start to look tentatively towards the future and begin to let go of the past.

However, all this takes time. Time can indeed be a great healer, but only when we are afforded the amount of time each of us requires. Some will reach the various stages in the grieving process sooner than others.

Some may do so within months rather than years. Some may consciously come to terms with their loss. Some may keep on telling themselves it was all a bad dream that happened to someone else, not to them. However we choose to handle our loss is up to us. A lot depends on the type of person we are, how much support we get from those around us, and on our life experiences before the loss.

Once we have plucked up the courage, we move on a little, but this often does not happen until we come to the understanding that we shall never forget the child we have lost. Others might, but we will not. This understanding allows us to be braver, while slowly but steadily moving on, and in due course we may be able to look back beyond our darkest days, months or years, and enjoy the happier memories of times we had with our child; and be able to say to ourselves: 'It was a privilege to have known them and to have had them share our lives'.